MADEMOISELLE DE LA BRINDILLE
TEXT: ANNE-CLAIRE LÉVÊQUE

HAPPY VOODOO GRIS GRIS

photographs: Fabrice Besse

NORTH LIGHT BOOKS

CINCINNATI, OHIO

To Gilberte and Hélène, my grandmothers, Brigitte, my mother,
Alix, Manon and Marin, my little nieces and the future creative talent of the family...
V. L.

For my sister Mirane, specialist in crystal-ball gazing!
A.-C. L.

Mademoiselle de la Brindille would like to thank

Valérie Gendreau for her patience and for loving my jewelry and without whom this book would never have seen the light of day. Anne-Claire and Lucas for being my friends and introducing me to India and Anne-Claire for embarking on this wonderful adventure with me.
Zoé for her pretty pictures and illustrations, her fresh approach and her inordinate love of pink whisky...
Fabrice for his beautiful photos and his great patience.
Sonia for having brought our work to light and Étienne for his artwork.
The entire Lefebvre family for their indispensable support ever since 'la Brindille' began.
Quentin, Alix, Austin, Marin and Manon for their photos.
Fleur, Arno, Éric, Anne and Bruno, Roxane, Isabelle, Catherine, Marie-Jo, Anya, Alain and Elena my friends... for their precious friendship.
Pauline, without whom my path wouldn't have been the same...
My editing friends, Anne, Sandrine, Aurélie and Colombine... for their support right from the outset.
Valérie for her layout, Camille, Laetitia, Louis, Morgane, Victoire and Victoria for their mischievous little faces, Guitch and Soleil for their magical presence.

Anne and La Droguerie for having introduced me to the magical world of beads as a child; Mokuba ribbons and Nancy for her faithful collaboration; Petit Bateau for their nightdresses; Bandaï for their clever badge and lucky charm machines; Rougier et Plé, a temple to DIY; DMC for their delightful threads and the sublime Bougies La Française candles.

Anne-Claire Lévêque would like to thank

Valérie Lefebvre who had faith in her text.
Anne Tricaud, curator at the Musée des Arts et Traditions Populaires who opened its collections especially for me (temporarily closed to the public).
The authors of the books that made up my reference bibliography when drafting the text of this book:
Amulettes et Talismans, coll. de L. Bonnemère, Réunion des Musées nationaux, 1991.
Les Porte-Bonheur, S. Paine, Alternatives, 2005.
Dictionnaire des symboles, J. Chevalier and A. Gheerbrant, coll. Bouquins, Robert Laffont/Jupiter, 1982.
La Sorcellerie en France aujourd'hui, D. Camus. Éd. Ouest-France, 2001.
Dictionnaires des symboles musulmans, M. Chebel, Albin Michel, 1995.
Lutins et Lutines, F. Morvan, Librio, 2002.
And also...
Philippe Bréson, Anne-Valérie Gaston, Michèle Lévêque, Catherine Stein, Axèle and Daniel Tricaud and Lucas Weinachter.

Manufactured in China.
First published in North America by
North Light Craft, an imprint of F+W Publications, 4700 East Galbraith Road, Cincinnati, OH 45236 • 800-289-0963

First published in France by Dessain et Tolra / Larousse

© Dessain et Tolra / Larousse 2006
ISBN-13: 978-1-60061-122-3

contents

Soleil, my parrot, spends his time on my shoulder or on my head and tries in vain to make off with beads or ribbons!

As a child, I wanted to be an interior decorator. I have been writing in the press about interior decoration for twelve years! A trip to India, five years ago, confirmed my wish to change my life: to invent jewelry for daydreaming, for having fun… I created my brand "Mademoiselle de la Brindille." When I was asked to publish a book, I wanted to expand my world as a creator of lucky-charm jewelry into imagining jeweled charms for the home.

MADEMOISELLE DE LA BRINDILL
JEWELRY-MAKER..

Colors

"Color has taken possession of me; no longer do I have to chase after it, I know that it has hold of me forever… Such is the reality of this blessed moment. Color and I are both one: I am a painter." I like this quotation by Paul Klee. It speaks to me!

Creative spirit: a family heritage!

My passion for decoration came from my grandmothers. One of them was a milliner with nimble fingers. The other liked flowers, birds and beetles: her walls were covered with boxes containing her best specimens! The exotic world in which she lived, surrounded by Chinese ornaments and items from the Ivory Coast, drew me towards other worlds. As for my mother, sometimes she was queen of crêpe paper flowers, sometimes princess of sewing or empress of collage; today, she is a sculptor. The "Mademoiselle de la Brindille" that I have become today owes a lot to all of them!

Jewelry

I'm captivated by the jewelry worn by people around the world. I draw my inspiration from it. It all started when I discovered the jewelry of the Maharajahs. Apart from its magnificence, I was fascinated by its symbolism: the personal astrologers of these Princes of India dictated the setting of these precious stones according to their birth chart. This is what influenced me to work with lucky charms, exotic charms and symbols of protection.

OR THE HOME!

Gems

A veritable coming together of materials, colors and properties with real or invented powers... It doesn't matter either way, what is important is to believe in it and to allow yourself to be filled with the magic.

Ribbons

Trimmings fascinate me. Few people appreciate the value of beautiful ribbons! I find them a real treasure.

Anne-Claire, my friend, likes to say that she's a sorceress…
A spot of magic transformed our relationship, which was initially professional, into a beautiful friendship. As a journalist and lover of words, her pen has traveled the four corners of the world, with a curiosity for other traditions. Lucas, her partner, is an artist, also passionate about jewelry. Over dinners filled with laughter, we discussed a trip to southern India, where we went for a month. This was all that I needed to ask her to write the text for this book.

"I couldn't live without books!" says Anne-Claire
"Novels, poetry, tales, documents, I choose them with care and eagerness, then I devour them and enjoy them even more one or two years later. My library is always in a state of change: I lend to my friends, I dig up a reference, I savor a chance page…"

My "things" according to Anne-Claire
"Whether it's something precious or simply well-worn, cheap bric-à-brac uncovered in unlikely markets – I've always brought things back from my travels! They speak to me more than a photo and remind me of a country, someone I met or a story. I appreciate their needlessness: they are happy to be just what they are."

REVEAL TH

WHAT IS AN AMULET?
IT'S AN OBJECT THAT CAN BE MADE FROM DIFFERENT ELEMENTS AND/OR MATERIALS (THREAD, STONES, SEEDS, FRAGMENTS OF ANIMALS, BEADS, MIRRORS, AND SO ON) COMBINED TOGETHER ACCORDING TO PRECISE RULES TO MAKE A MAGIC "SHIELD" TO WARD OFF EVIL SPIRITS AND THE EVIL EYE. MOST AMULETS ARE RECOGNIZED WORLDWIDE; ONLY SOME OF THEM ARE SPECIFIC TO CERTAIN CULTURES. IT CAN BE A SIMPLE BLUE BEAD OR A COLLECTION OF MIRRORS AND RED THREAD…

BONHEUR · VEINE · PROSPÉRITÉ · LONGÉVITÉ · LE LANGAGE DES PORTE-BONHEUR

WHAT IS A CHARM?
THIS OBJECT DOES NOT PROTECT, BUT IT ATTRACTS LUCK, BRINGS HAPPINESS AND GOOD HEALTH (FOR EXAMPLE A HORSESHOE OR A FOUR-LEAFED CLOVER).

ORIGIN, SIGNIFICANCE AND POWER: MEANING BEHIND LUCKY CHARMS

Jewelry from Mademoiselle de la Brindille is inspired by customs and amulets from around the world designed to protect your home or those you love…

Each creation is accompanied by a note for you to "digest" and discover its symbolism and power.

WHAT IS A TALISMAN?
IT'S AN OBJECT THAT POSSESSES SUPERNATURAL POWERS. IT PROTECTS AND EXERCISES A MAGIC POWER. IT CAN BE USED DURING RITUALS.

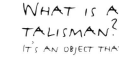

air

eArth

water

natUre

MY OUTDOOR LUCKY CHARMS
INSPIRATIONS...

To want to protect your home and its surroundings is a natural desire; you don't want to risk the intrusion of evil spirits! Whether it's a simple box, a sacred edifice or even a yurt, there are many protective symbols to choose from: motifs painted around the windows, a hanging to protect your entrance hall or even a horseshoe or a cross…

A traditional house in Toraja, on the island of Sulawesi... Horns are well-known amulets in many parts of the world, as their tapering points are capable of piercing evil spirits.

In the Muslim world, the entrance to the house is protected by painted hand imprints. They symbolize the hand of Fatima, who thus extends her powers to all those in the household.

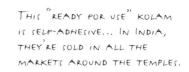

This "ready for use" kolam is self-adhesive... In India, they're sold in all the markets around the temples.

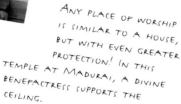

Any place of worship is similar to a house, but with even greater protection! In this temple at Madurai, a divine benefactress supports the ceiling.

On flicking through an Indian national daily paper... an advert illustrated with a picture of a kolam.

வண்ணக்கோலம்

இந்த வார வண்ணக் கோலத்துக்காக
25 பரிசு பெறுபவர்:-சி.ராஜேஸ்வரி,
க்கு மாடவீதி, வடபழனி, சென்னை-26.
(கோலம்: 11-1 நேர்புள்ளி)

This tree of life cut out of paper comes from Poland. In Catholic parts of Europe it symbolizes the tree of knowledge, original sin and the hope of redemption.

a protective kolam

CUT FLOWERS ARE ALSO SOMETIMES SCATTERED OVER THE KOLAM TO MAKE IT LOOK EVEN NICER AND TO STRENGTHEN THE POWER...

The art of kolam traditionally exists in several regions in southern India. This design is traced on the ground in front of the entrance to the house, as well as beneath representations of divinities. Made with rice flour and colored powder, the kolam honors the goddess Lakshmi, who represents wealth and beauty. This design will therefore bring luck and prosperity to the inhabitants of the house.

As a welcome sign for visitors, its decorative aspect is a pleasure to behold!

You will need...
- **paper**
- **a box of colored crayons**
- **chalk (large and small) in light blue, turquoise and green**

1. First of all, design a motif in colored crayons on a sheet of paper using the example for inspiration.

2. Start by using the small chalks to draw the center of the design on your doorstep, then work around it to enlarge the motifs as you go, mixing the colors. Use the large chalks to fill in the motifs.

3. Extend the motif to the edge of the door and the steps of your staircase to expand your design, and then encourage the gods to come into your home.

door charms

From North to South, throughout the world, the doors to houses have always been defended by charms or amulets to prevent demons from entering.

Antlers or horns above the entrance, horseshoes, paintings of symbols on the wall or a raised threshold… Every country has its own customs!

These hanging charms take their inspiration from the four elements: water, air, earth and fire.

AMULETS IN THE SHAPE OF A TRIANGLE ARE VERY COMMON. THIS SHAPE SYMBOLIZES THE NUMBER 3 ("HEAVEN, EARTH AND HELL" OR "FATHER, MOTHER AND CHILD" OR, OF COURSE, THE TRINITY: "FATHER, SON AND HOLY GHOST").

THESE TRIANGLES ARE FOUND IN AMULETS THAT DECORATE DOORS, AS WELL AS IN THE FORM OF JEWELRY, EMBROIDERED MOTIFS AND SCAPULARS CONTAINING A PRAYER OR SALT…

14

Air charms

You will need…

- **a small lampshade frame in a fun shape**
- **approx. 20 feathers in different sizes**
- **5 glass or crystal pendants from a flea market**
- **a small, blown-glass bird with a claw (look in your boxes of Christmas decorations, there's bound to be one there…)**
- **2 yd. of white organza ribbon in 1/4 in. width**
- **1 1/2 yd. of white organza ribbon in 1 1/2 in. width**

1. Make four little bunches of feathers that you can attach using the fine organza ribbon. Allow a length of around 6 in. to attach them to the shade.

2. Attach each pendant to a ribbon. Allow a length of around 6 in. to attach them to the frame.

3. Alternate the feathers and the pendants all around the shade.

4. Attach the wide ribbon so that it conceals the ring designed to hang the shade and allow 1 yd. of ribbon to attach it to your door.

5. Finally, once you have fixed your charm to the door, find the nicest place to attach your glass bird.

THE FEATHERS THAT I USED CAME FROM SOLEIL, MY PARROT.

THEY ARE SO BEAUTIFUL THAT I ALWAYS COLLECT THEM WHEN HE MOLTS.

THEY SYMBOLIZE THE AIR AND IMMORTALITY. LIKE THOSE USED BY SORCERERS AND SHAMANS.

Earth charms

You will need…

- **1 plastic elephant and 1 plastic bear**
- **1 large bead made from exotic wood**
- **ribbons in all widths and in different colors**
- **1 nail**
- **1 hammer**

1. Cut a long piece of ribbon and wind one end 3 times around the body of the elephant to hold it in place. Tie a knot and slide the exotic wood bead on to the two ribbons and tie another knot.

2. Cut a long ribbon and wind it in the same way around the body of the bear. Tie a knot at the stomach.

3. Take the two ribbons, place the bear under the elephant and make a loop at the other end of the ribbons.

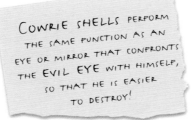

COWRIE SHELLS PERFORM THE SAME FUNCTION AS AN EYE OR MIRROR THAT CONFRONTS THE EVIL EYE WITH HIMSELF, SO THAT HE IS EASIER TO DESTROY!

Sea charms

You will need…

- **4 plastic fish**
- **2 largish pieces of driftwood**
- **3 cowrie shells**
- **ribbons in all widths and in different colors**
- **cotton cord in brown and beige**
- **1 aluminium tube (for example a cigar tube)**
- **1 gimlet**

THE NATIVE AMERICAN DREAM-CATCHERS, MADE FROM A NET AND FEATHERS, ARE REPUTED TO CAPTURE EVIL SPIRITS AND HELP ENCOURAGE GOOD DREAMS.

1. Attach a fish to a ribbon, then a cowrie shell and then a second fish. Cut a piece of beige cord and attach the third fish. Fix the fourth fish to a ribbon. Hang a cowrie shell on to the brown cord.

2. Pierce each piece of driftwood using the gimlet so that the cord and ribbons can be slipped through. Pierce the cork and the aluminium tube too using the gimlet.

3. Arrange the fish and cowrie shells on the driftwood, together with the tube, sliding the ribbons through the holes. Make a loop in the cord for hanging the charm. Don't forget to slip a message, a proverb or whatever words have meaning for you into the tube.

Fire charms

You will need...

- a 6¼ in. square of red silk
- 1 rectangle of coated canvas in fuchsia, 8 x 4 in.
- embroidery thread in fuchsia pink
- nylon thread
- 1 needle
- ribbons in fuchsia
- 7 mother-of-pearl buttons in different diameters, 1 freshwater pearl, 2 red glass beads, 1 piece of coral, 1 plastic salamander
- cotton wool
- 1 chain link in copper color
- 1 tube of red acrylic paint
- 1 paintbrush
- 2 pieces of card (2¼ x 8 in.)

1. Fold the square of red silk to make a triangle. Sew together and stuff with cotton wool, closing the remaining gap.

2. Cut two irregular flowers from the coated canvas. Attach them to the triangle with a mother-of-pearl button.

3. Paint the salamander red. Attach it to one of the ribbons, adding some mother-of-pearl buttons in different sizes.

4. To make each of the tassels, wrap the skein of embroidery cotton around the rectangle of card, lengthways. Tie a knot and then remove the card. Make the head of the tassel 1¼ in. from the top and trim the ends at the bottom.

5. Arrange buttons and beads on the ribbons using the example as an illustration.

6. Attach the decorations to the triangle as in the photo. Sew on the large red ribbon: this is what you will use to attach the charm to your door.

a wishing fountain

Water is life… It regenerates and purifies, it also symbolizes subconscious energies and secret motivations. Water, which is precious to us all, is at the heart of religions, myths and legends, where it is given sacred or magic powers. All places of worship or pilgrimage have fountains. Money or safety pins are thrown into them to make a wish come true or to cure an illness.

You will need…

- **an old zinc basin**
- **1 Buddha and his rosary**
- **1 large, plastic goldfish**
- **pebbles**
- **silver leaf**
- **a bottle of compound for sticking the leaves**
- **a paintbrush**
- **a large basin to stand your creation in, or any other support…**
- **4 bamboo sticks**
- **a sari**
- **lotus flowers made from fabric**
- **safety pins**
- **candles, including floating ones**
- **party lights for a touch of magic**

Silvered pebbles

Clean your pebbles. Dry them. Using a brush, apply the compound to one end of the pebble. Wait 15 minutes. Randomly tear up a piece of silver leaf, stick it on to the glue. Smooth it with your finger. Repeat the process on as many pebbles as you wish.

Positioning

1. Put your little basin into the large one. Fill the basin with pebbles. Place the Buddha and the goldfish a suitable distance apart on the pebbles. Fill the basin with water. Place some floating candles on the water.

2. Slightly behind, stick four bamboo sticks into the ground to hold your canopy. Tie the sari to the rear bamboos, starting at the left, then

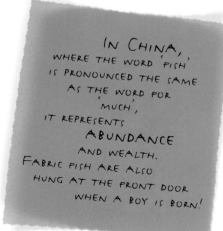

IN CHINA, WHERE THE WORD 'FISH' IS PRONOUNCED THE SAME AS THE WORD FOR 'MUCH', IT REPRESENTS ABUNDANCE AND WEALTH. FABRIC FISH ARE ALSO HUNG AT THE FRONT DOOR WHEN A BOY IS BORN!

wind it around the bamboo sticks from right to left. Let the fabric hang down on the left. Use safety pins to hold the sari in place and balance it. Arrange the party lights over the sari and around the canopy.

3. Place fabric flowers and candles around the foot of the large basin. Warning: never leave your candles unattended, and remember to unplug the party lights at the end of the evening. Don't forget to use lights designed for exterior use.

When night falls, just take your friends to your fountain and let their hearts speak to them… they can throw in coins from their travels around the world.

THE FISH IS THE WATER CREATURE THAT HAS THE MOST SYMBOLIC VALUE. IT MOVES AROUND IN TOTAL FREEDOM AND SYMBOLIZES FERTILITY, MAKING IT AN ESSENTIAL AMULET! YOU'LL FIND THEM EMBROIDERED ON WOMEN'S CLOTHES IN TUNISIA, AND A BERBER LEGEND SAYS THAT A FISH SHOULD BE PLACED ON THE THRESHOLD OF THE BRIDE'S FUTURE HOME BEFORE SHE CROSSES IT.

The tree is a powerful symbol. Its roots plunge into the ground, its branches rise towards the sky; it's the axis of the world! Its continual regeneration symbolizes victory over death and the cycle of life. It is the tree of nourishment.

To chase away the evil eye and increase protection around the boundaries of your home, a tree mobile can be very effective, as well as pretty.

THE POWER OF THE TREE IS PRESENT IN ITS BRANCHES, ITS LEAVES, ITS TRUNK OR ITS FRUITS THAT WE REMOVE TO USE FOR PROTECTION.

IN RUSSIA, IT IS CUSTOMARY TO PROTECT YOUR HOUSE WITH A PIECE OF BIRCH BARK.

IN AFRICA, TWIGS TIED WITH RED RAG PROTECT AGAINST THIEVES AND VAMPIRES. IN EUROPE, WE "TOUCH WOOD" TO BRING US LUCK.

20

a mobile in the trees

You will need…
- **a mobile in bamboo**
- **ribbons in all widths and in different colors**
- **lots of little bells, in all sizes and colors and in various types**
- **small mirrors pre-cut for sticking**
- **silver sequins in different sizes**
- **very strong glue**
- **a pair of scissors**
- **a mini-drill or a gimlet**

1. Make sure you take a good look at the different fixings on your mobile before removing them! Make each hole bigger using the drill or gimlet. Replace each fixing with ribbons. Choose them in different colors, to make it brighter.

2. Drill some new holes in the bottom of the tubes so that you can attach extra bells. As you attach the tubes to the base, slip some bells on to the ribbons. Stick mirrors on to ribbons, leave to dry flat and then hang them on to the mobile. Stick several little mirrors on to the bamboo too. It's best to do this with the mobile laid down to prevent any of the little mirrors from slipping before they are dry.

3. Balance up the mobile as you go along. Have fun decorating the mobile as much as you like: the more bells, the nicer the sound and it will be more effective, too! Now all you have to do is hang it up…

MY WELCOMING
LUCKY CHARMS

MY WELCOMING LUCKY CHARMS

INSPIRATIONS...

The etiquette of hospitality is different depending on where in the world you are, but for all of us the desire is the same: to honor our guests with a warm welcome.

A welcoming home is a place where you feel good. So why not adopt some customs designed to bring good luck?

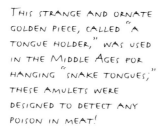

THIS STRANGE AND ORNATE GOLDEN PIECE, CALLED "A TONGUE HOLDER," WAS USED IN THE MIDDLE AGES FOR HANGING "SNAKE TONGUES;" THESE AMULETS WERE DESIGNED TO DETECT ANY POISON IN MEAT!

THIS LINGUAM, VENERATED IN ONE OF THE TEMPLES AT CHENNAI (IN THE SOUTH OF INDIA), IS DECORATED WITH FRESH FLOWER GARLANDS AS AN OFFERING.

RITUAL OFFERINGS AT THE ENTRANCE TO A BUDDHIST TEMPLE AT PHNOM PENH, IN CAMBODIA: HARMONY AND GENTLENESS...

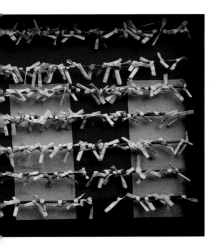

IN THIS SANCTUARY IN TOKYO, JAPAN, BELIEVERS HANG THEIR WRITTEN WISHES ON STRIPS OF WHITE PAPER. THE COLOR IS ASSOCIATED WITH THE WHITE LOTUS FLOWER AND WITH THE "FIST OF KNOWLEDGE" IN JAPANESE BUDDHISM.

THIS PIOUS IMAGE FROM THE END OF THE 19TH CENTURY PAYS HOMAGE TO THE WORSHIP OF THE SACRED HEART OF JESUS. MOST OF THESE PICTURES WERE CAREFULLY PRESERVED AND CONSIDERED AS AMULETS BY MANY CATHOLICS AT THE TIME.

SACRÉ-CŒUR DE JESUS
SOURCE DE TOUTE MISERICORDE

THE TEMPLE OF SETO MACHENDRANATH, DEDICATED TO BUDDHIST AND HINDU WORSHIP, IS ONE OF THE OLDEST IN KATHMANDU (NEPAL). ITS BELL IS VENERATED BY THE TIBETANS, FOR WHOM IT SYMBOLIZES WISDOM AND THE "PHENOMENAL" WORLD (IN THE EYES OF THE WORLD OF APPEARANCES).

V.F.C.A.

THIS NAIVE COMMEMORATIVE PLAQUE, CREATED BY AN ANONYMOUS PAINTER IN NAPLES IN 1856, IS AN OFFERING DESIGNED TO DECORATE A CHURCH, BY WAY OF A THANK-YOU TO THE VIRGIN MARY, WHO GRANTED A WISH TO BE CURED.

IN SOUTH AMERICA, IT'S QUITE COMMON TO FIND ALTARS TO THE VIRGIN MARY, JESUS CHRIST OR THE SAINTS INSIDE PEOPLE'S APARTMENTS.

an unusual center light

We all know the tradition of exchanging kisses under the mistletoe to bring happiness…

This center light is less ephemeral, yet more fun and constantly changing, with its unusual pendants that will welcome everyone who comes to see you. Kiss them and they will bring other talismans to add to your mobile!

PORTE BONHEUR

THE HORSESHOE COMBINES THE TALISMAN-LIKE POWER OF IRON (WHICH IS USED FOR POINTED TOOLS THAT "PIERCE" EVIL SPIRITS) AND THE HORSE (A FAVOURABLE ANIMAL) WITH A CRESCENT SHAPE THAT EVOKES FERTILITY.

You will need…
- **7 circles of copper wire 2mm in thickness and 15³/₄ in. in diameter**
- **ribbons in all widths and in different colors**
- **pendants in different sizes**

1. Make the shape of the center light using the copper wire: start by counting the number of circles – you will need seven (a highly symbolic number…). Take four of them in your left hand and three in your right hand. Insert the three in your right hand into the circles in your left hand and attach them straight away by grouping them together using one end of the metal and a piece of ribbon. Then, raise and separate the circles to form unequal, round spheres that are elegantly arranged.

2. Hang all your pendants in various places, so that your center light looks prettily decorated from whichever way you look at it. Now all you have to do is find your partner and kiss them under the center light. So, close your eyes and make a wish…

27

a mini-temple

By the edge of a road in Greece, at a hairdresser's in Bali, in a taxi in Rio or in the corner of a lounge in Russia…

These "altars" of fortune, whether sacred or magical, are found all around the world. Whether they are dedicated to icons, divinities or protective saints, it's a way of paying homage and of associating them with the events of daily life, bringing happiness and luck.

This composition, freely inspired by these mini-temples, will display the treasures that you love, like a precious Baroque display cabinet.

OUR LADY OF LOURDES, THE VIRGIN MARY, IS OMNIPRESENT IN PIOUS IMAGERY AND SOMETIMES REPRESENTED IN THE SHAPE OF A HEART.

SAINT ANTHONY OF PADUA IS THE MOST INVOKED IN TERMS OF PROTECTION. SAINT ROCH IS SAID TO HAVE DIVINE POWER OVER CONTAGIOUS DISEASES.

You will need…

- a frame found in a second-hand shop
- pious images, icons, representations of divinities (Indian gods, Buddha, the Virgin Mary and so on)
- an angel, a fairy, a tiny bird, a tiny mushroom (decoration from a Japanese bonsai garden), a little tiger, a butterfly button in mother-of-pearl, a horseshoe, a metal star, a mother-of-pearl rosary, a little bell, a fabric flower…
- religious symbols, crosses from all religions, a hand of Fatima…
- some pink and orange glass beads
- nylon thread
- rings and drawing pins
- white glue and wood glue
- ribbons in all widths and in different colors
- 4 clamps
- small nails

- a hammer
- a paintbrush
- water-based wood primer and water-based paint in lilac
- a large turquoise candle, a small aniseed candle
- an X-ACTO knife
- a pencil

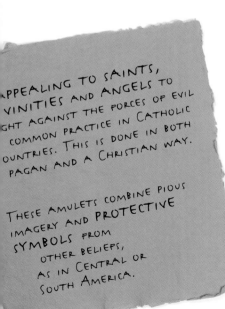

APPEALING TO SAINTS, DIVINITIES AND ANGELS TO FIGHT AGAINST THE FORCES OF EVIL IS COMMON PRACTICE IN CATHOLIC COUNTRIES. THIS IS DONE IN BOTH A PAGAN AND A CHRISTIAN WAY.

THESE AMULETS COMBINE PIOUS IMAGERY AND PROTECTIVE SYMBOLS FROM OTHER BELIEFS, AS IN CENTRAL OR SOUTH AMERICA.

Making the temple

1. Cut planks of wood 0.5 mm thick to make a display cabinet the shape of your frame (you will need 4 sides and one backing piece). Remember to measure your statues before cutting the wood. Stick the sides together. Fix with the clamp and leave to dry for 4 hours. Nail the sides together to strengthen the framework. Nail on the back of the display cabinet.

2. Paint the box (inside and out) with the primer (two coats). Then paint the inside of the box in lilac.

3. The following day, attach the back to the picture frame using wood glue.

Decorating the inside of the temple

1. Place your statues in the temple. Stick on your pictures, arranging them nicely inside and on the sides.

2. Prepare a horseshoe on a little ribbon loop and a star decorated with a mother-of-pearl rosary. Pin them on to the sides.

Decorating the outside of the temple

The garland of religious symbols: thread the religious symbols, crosses, stars and the like on to the pink ribbon and attach it to the frame using drawing pins. Don't draw the ribbon too tight and it will look nicer.

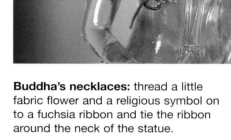

Buddha's necklaces: thread a little fabric flower and a religious symbol on to a fuchsia ribbon and tie the ribbon around the neck of the statue.

For the rosary: thread on beads and a little bell. Attach the thread to two rings and the two rings to a piece of suedette ribbon.

The angel: attach a heart to the neck of the angel using a fuchsia ribbon and attach the angel to the top at the center of the frame using a drawing pin.

THE HAND OF FATIMA, A RELIGIOUS SYMBOL, REPRESENTS WITH ITS FIVE FINGERS THE FIVE DOCTRINES OF ISLAM. THE PROTECTION IT PROVIDES AGAINST THE EVIL EYE IS SUCH THAT ITS MOTIF IS REPRODUCED IN EMBROIDERY ON CLOTHES, ON DOOR KNOCKERS AND SO ON.

The fairy: attach the bird and the mushroom to each hand of the fairy. Attach a religious symbol on a fuchsia ribbon around the neck of the fairy, then slip the butterfly button on to the ribbon. Tie a knot and attach the fairy to one of the two drawing pins at the end of the garland.

The tiger and its religious symbol: decorate the tiger with a religious symbol and hang it on a little fuchsia ribbon, and attach it to the other drawing pin on the garland, opposite the fairy.

The candles

All temples have candles. Carve strong symbols like the Aum (sacred mantra) or the wind (Chinese ideogram) around the edge of your candles.

1. Draw your symbols on to each of the candles using a pencil.

2. Redraw the motif and scoop out the thin layer of wax using the point of the X-ACTO.

3. Run the candle under warm water to clean it and smooth the wax within the motif.

a table runner

Embroidered hangings, fabrics or simple mats are often placed by fireplaces or windows. This is because these apertures need to be protected from intrusion by evil spirits. The weaving, which intertwines the threads, plays its role in scaring away demons and the evil eye; embroidery and ornamentation reinforce this power. Horns, eight-pointed stars, triangles, the tree of life, the eye and the hand are the most well-known favourable symbols.
Borrow them to make a table runner that will bring you good luck!

I LOVE FABRICS;
I'VE GOT THEM EVERYWHERE,
HUNG, TORN, FOLDED...

THEY REMIND ME
OF SPECIFIC MOMENTS.

I USE THEM A LOT WITH
MY JEWELRY.
SO, DO THE SAME AS ME,
HAVE A RUMMAGE THROUGH
YOUR WARDROBES!

You will need…
- **a strip of striped fabric 5½ in. wide**
- **a strip of plain fabric 10½ in. wide**
- **little scraps of fabric for the motifs**
- **15¾ in. of double-sided adhesive fabric**
- **1 can of repositionable glue**
- **3¾ yd. of green ribbon**
- **sewing thread in turquoise**
- **embroidery thread in fuchsia**
- **a needle with a large eye**
- **a box of pins**
- **a pair of scissors**
- **some sheets of paper and a crayon to create your motifs, or the cut-out templates**
- **an iron**
- **a damp cloth**

More fun than traditional table runners, these are covered with strips of fabric and decorated with symbols and meaningful words.

For the striped edging

1. Turn under edge and machine-stitch a border along the fabric to make a perfect edging.

2. Choose words that are important to you and write them freehand using the green ribbon, by folding the ribbon to form the shape of the letters and pinning on with the pins as you go along.

3. For some letters, you will have to cut the pieces of ribbon and make joins. To do so, fold the ribbon and always slip the raw edge underneath so that it doesn't fray over time.

4. Machine-stitch the letters in place.

IN MANY COUNTRIES,
AMULETS ARE HUNG ON TO
WEAVING LOOMS
TO PREVENT EVIL SPIRITS
FROM SABOTAGING
THE WORK IN PROGRESS!

13!

A NUMBER HONORED SINCE ANTIQUITY, WHICH CAN BE INTERPRETED AS A BAD SIGN (THE KABBALAH LISTS 13 EVIL SPIRITS) OR, ALTERNATIVELY, CAN BE CONSIDERED TO BE THE MOST POWERFUL NUMBER AND THE MOST SUBLIME (ZEUS AND HIS 12 GODS).

NUMBER 13 WAS FUNDAMENTAL IN ASTRONOMY AND THE CALENDAR FOR THE AZTECS: A WEEK LASTED 13 DAYS. AS THIS NUMBER CORRESPONDED TO A NEW BEGINNING, PLAYERS MADE IT THEIR FAVORITE NUMBER.

I HAVE USED A SARI IN TURQUOISE COTTON HERE, A SOUVENIR OF A FABULOUS TRIP TO INDIA. IT'S EASY AS THERE IS NO NEED TO MAKE A HEM.

THE COTTON WILL ALWAYS LOOK GOOD, EVEN IF IT FRAYS A LITTLE, AND THE GOLDEN BORDER WILL ALWAYS STAY PERFECT! I HAVE CHOSEN SYMBOLS THAT I LIKE BOTH FOR THEIR GRAPHIC NATURE AND FOR THEIR SYMBOLISM: A SALAMANDER, A PEONY, A HAND OF FATIMA, THE NUMBER 13 AND A GINKGO BILOBA LEAF.

34

For the "sari" strip

1. Photocopy the templates (p. 34), enlarging them to the size that you need. Cut them out. You will use them on the reverse side to cut out the motifs from the fabric.

2. Paste your templates with repositionable glue, place your motif on the fabric and cut closely around it.

3. Repeat the process on the adhesive fabric and cut out slightly smaller than the fabric motifs, so that you cannot see the white underneath.

4. Place your fabric on the adhesive motif and, once you have chosen the right place on the sari, iron on with a very hot iron and a damp cloth.

The "Abracadabra" embroidery
1. Cut out a rectangle of plain blue fabric 31 cm by 9 cm.

2. Thread an embroidery needle with fuchsia thread. Embroider the magic spell freehand in large stitches. Don't worry if the stitching isn't perfect, it will just add charm to your runner and emphasize the spell!

ABRACADABRA

ONE OF THE GREAT WRITTEN AMULETS, THIS FAMOUS SPELL COMES FROM THE HEBREW "ABREQ AD HÂDRA" (HURL YOUR THUNDERBOLT EVEN UNTO DEATH). WRITTEN ON NEW FABRIC, FORMING AN UPSIDE-DOWN TRIANGLE, IT SENDS BAD ENERGY TO THE BOTTOM WHERE IT IS "DRAGGED DOWN" BY THE FUNNEL TO BE CONQUERED AND CURED.

ABRACADABRA
ABRACADABR
ABRACADAB
ABRACADA
ABRACAD
ABRACA
ABRAC
ABRA
ABR
AB
A

a rosary for the home

Designed and created to reflect rosaries used for prayer, this decoration for the home is hung on a wall. And as an everlasting rosary, it is a reflection of the many customs around the world that combine seeds and beneficial plants to ward off the devil, witches or vampires.

You will need…

- **ribbons in all widths and in different colors**
- **2 pieces of raw silk: one 4 x 6 in. in fuchsia, the other 3 x 3¹/₂ in. in yellowy green**
- **pins, a small safety pin**
- **1 metal ring 1.5 cm in diameter**
- **beads and buttons in all sizes and colors**
- **2 peppers in resin, 1 fabric flower, 1 smiling Buddha, 1 cross**
- **spices and seeds (Indian rosary lotus, star anise, cinnamon, cloves…)**

CLOVES, COMBINED WITH SAFFRON AND MUSK, ARE ALSO CONSIDERED TO BE EXCELLENT FOR REPELLING DJINNS (SPIRITS).

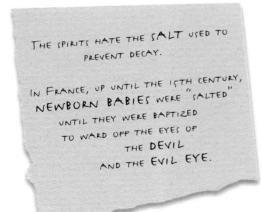

THE SPIRITS HATE THE SALT USED TO PREVENT DECAY.

IN FRANCE, UP UNTIL THE 15TH CENTURY, NEWBORN BABIES WERE "SALTED" UNTIL THEY WERE BAPTIZED TO WARD OFF THE EYES OF THE DEVIL AND THE EVIL EYE.

Preparing the structure

1. Attach your Buddha to the bundle of cinnamon using a ribbon. Thread beads and ribbons on to the two strands of ribbon. Thread the lotus seeds and star anise on to another ribbon. Attach them to the metal ring.

2. Fold a 4 yd. ribbon in half and attach it to the ring. Thread beads and buttons on to each strand, varying the colors and shapes. Tie the two strands to one another to make a loop big enough to hang up the rosary.

Making the pouches

Make the two silk pouches that will hold salt, garlic and a potpourri of scented flowers.
Perhaps even a secret charm of your choice!

1. For each pouch, fold over the edges of the square of fabric twice to make a neat seam, fix with pins and stitch.
Fold the two edges (widthways) inwards and fix with pins. Make a 1/8 in. seam around the edge, so that the little ribbon can be slipped through to close the pouch. Fold the fabric in half, edge to edge, and stitch the edges together lengthways.

2. Cut two pieces of fine ribbon and, using the safety pin, slip them through each of the top edges of the pouch; finish by tying together in a knot. Take one of the strands of ribbon from the rosary, attach the safety pin to it and slide the ribbon into one of the edges of the first pouch. Attach a little orange bead and a pink resin pepper and finish off with a double knot. Do the same with the second strand and the second pouch.

a wishing tree

In Japan, Tanabata, "the festival of stars," is celebrated on July 7th. This is when the Japanese write wishes on strips of paper in five different colors and hang them on to trees so that their wishes will come true.

Make the pleasure last with this tree, which will grant your wishes throughout the year!

IN CHINA, CHERRY TREE BLOSSOM IS CONSIDERED TO BE THE PRINCESS OF ALL FLOWERS. WHILE ITS BEAUTY AND TRANSLUCENT WHITENESS REPRESENT INNOCENCE AND PURITY, ITS EARLY FLOWERING IS ALSO A SYMBOL OF LONGEVITY.

IT IS OFTEN GIVEN AS A WEDDING GIFT.

You will need…
- **a cherry tree branch or branch from any other flowering tree**
- **a piece of white linen**
- **some white chiffon ribbon**
- **some white, sequined braid**
- **2 sheets of white tracing paper**
- **2 sheets of iridescent paper**
- **a pair of scissors**
- **a felt pen**

1. Cut out strips in different widths from the white paper. Write your dearest wishes on them. They will remain secret, but will very likely come true… if you hang them up, of course.

2. Cut irregular strips from the white linen. Attach them in various places on the flowering branch to decorate it how you wish.

3. Likewise, cut ribbons from the chiffon in different widths and lengths and attach them to the tree.

4. Roll your strips of paper very tight. Cut some ribbon and tie a knot to prevent the rolls of paper from unravelling and attach them to the tree amongst the linen and chiffon ribbons.

a garland of happiness

More original than a forgotten family album, this garland running along the wall will depict all the precious moments you've spent with your family.

Funny or tender photos, tiny objects, air tickets, show tickets or little messages… they are all lovely memories. Everybody will want to continue to add to the garland, with love and good humor.

Happiness breeds happiness!

Choose a wall and measure it.
Adjust the width and length of your ribbons to fit.

You will need...

- **grosgrain in turquoise**
- **embroidery thread in aniseed, violet and marigold**
- **buttons, rings, and so on**
- **turquoise thread and 1 needle**
- **1 box of pins**
- **some fun pegs**
- **transparent plastic sheeting**
- **a pair of scissors**
- **1 sewing machine**

1. Make around ten plastic pockets in different sizes (think what they will need to hold and adjust their shapes accordingly) as follows: cut out some rectangles and some squares from the plastic, fold them in half and secure with pins to prevent the plastic from slipping, and top-stitch with the machine using turquoise thread.

2. Sew the pockets on to the ribbons using colored thread.

3. Fill the garland with all your treasures: family photos, little messages, drawings, favorite pebbles and brooches – in short, all your wonderful memories!

nest

love

softness

dream

MY SECRET LUCKY CHARMS

INSPIRATIONS...

Some charms come from a sacred place, drawing their pow
from a particular shape or a strong symbol...
These talismans evoke secret rituals. You too can create
revered objects and imagine your magic ritual.

CHILDREN ARE PARTICULARLY VULNERABLE TO EVIL SPIRITS! THIS LITTLE DAYAK BOY FROM THE BUNAQ TRIBE (ISLAND OF BORNEO) IS WEARING A HAT DECORATED WITH AMULETS, DESIGNED TO PROTECT HIM.

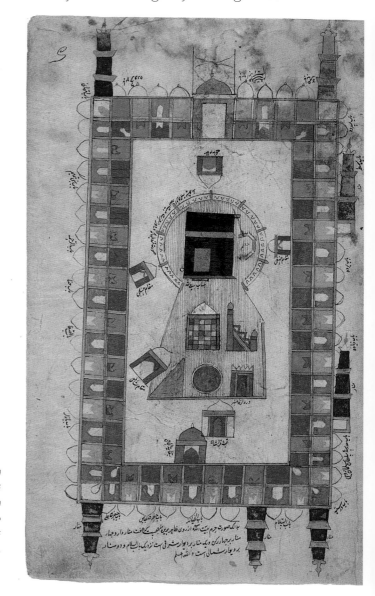

THIS MINIATURE PERSIAN RUG FROM THE 14TH CENTURY REPRESENTS KAABA, THE CENTER OF THE SANCTUARY OF THE MOSQUE AT MECCA, WHICH CONTAINS A METEORITE STONE. SOME PILGRIMS OWNED AMULETS CONTAINING DUST COLLECTED AROUND THE KAABA THAT THEY HUNG IN THEIR HOUSES.

IN JAPAN, BATHING IS A PURIFICATION RITUAL, AS IN MANY CIVILIZATIONS.

SCHEHERAZADE, THE LEGENDARY PRINCESS OF THE "ARABIAN NIGHTS," REPRESENTS FEMINI,NE SENSUALITY AND SEDUCTION.

THE VIRGIN MARY IS SOMETIMES REPRESENTED BY A HEART. THIS ONE HAS BEEN MADE FOR A GATHERING (FOR PRAYER) IN HER HONOR. THE YOUNG FIANCÉE, WHO KEPT THIS HEART AS AN AMULET, HAD ADDED A PRAYER TO ASK THE VIRGIN MARY FOR PROTECTION OF HER BETROTHED, HELD PRISONER IN GERMANY.

a scented burner

The imperceptible, yet real, subtlety of a perfume makes it symbolically similar to a spiritual presence and the soul. Its endurance, particularly in terms of the scent of a loved one, evokes the notion of duration and memories.

Among the most appreciated fragrances, sensual amber has a prized place.
Like the balls of Moroccan amber, this scented burner will add a touch of sophistication to the "Arabian Nights" decor in your bedroom.

ACCORDING TO POPULAR BELIEF, A MAN WHO BEARS AN AMBER OBJECT WILL NOT BE LET DOWN BY HIS VIRILITY!

You will need…

- **4 packets of pink, fluorescent Fimo (soft) paste**
- **a pointed kitchen knife with a smooth blade**
- **a wooden skewer**
- **a sheet of wax paper**
- **a piece of tissue paper**
- **some amber resin crystals (to burn)**

Inspired by balls of Moroccan amber, this great lotus flower will diffuse the subtle scent of amber throughout your home.

1. Knead the four packets of paste for some time until they are very malleable. Shape into a cylinder 1 1/2 in. high by 1 1/2 in. wide with a closed end. It will be the receptacle for the amber.

2. Make 7 lotus flower petals (using the shape of artichoke leaves as a guideline). Apply the 7 leaves one by one on top of one another to completely cover the cylinder and bend them slightly outwards.

3. Make 6 smaller petals and apply them one by one to the inside of the cylinder, turning them inwards.

4. Smooth the outside and inside of the flower. Reposition the petals if they fall off. Using a wooden skewer, pierce the base of the petals with some holes. The holes are designed to allow the amber fragrance to escape.

5. Using a small ball of paste, make a "hat" which doesn't completely fit. The imperfection will make it even more quirky.

6. Heat your oven to 250°F (130°C) and fire the flower and its hat (placed to one side) for around 25 minutes. Remove the rack from the oven and leave everything to cool before shaping your flower.

7. Wrap the pieces of amber in a piece of tissue paper and slip them inside your flower.

AMBER HAS THE POWER TO EMIT A SLIGHT ELECTRICAL IMPULSE AND AN INIMITABLE PERFUME WHEN YOU RUB IT.

AMBER ROSARIES AND AMULETS HAVE THE POWER TO RELEASE FROM THEIR EXCESSES THOSE WHO SAY THE ROSARY OR CARRY THEM.

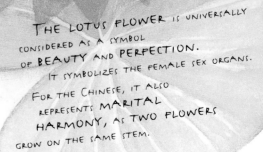

THE LOTUS FLOWER IS UNIVERSALLY CONSIDERED AS A SYMBOL OF BEAUTY AND PERFECTION. IT SYMBOLIZES THE FEMALE SEX ORGANS.

FOR THE CHINESE, IT ALSO REPRESENTS MARITAL HARMONY, AS TWO FLOWERS GROW ON THE SAME STEM.

a book of dreams

Unlock the secret of your dreams! Keep this at arm's reach by your bed: a book for noting your dreams, and discovering the meaning of your most secret desires.

The bookmark

1. Photocopy the template of the dragon (p. 80), and enlarge it so that it is slightly smaller than the size of a page of your book.

2. Place it on the metallic paper, trace the outline and the inside of the dragon, pressing down well using a lead pencil. Remove the sheet, go over all the edges and the inside design using pressure. Cut out the dragon.

Contrary to popular belief, the dragon isn't necessarily a demonic symbol, unless it is identified with a snake (like the najas who watch over the temples at Angkor). It doesn't represent evil, but instead defends a treasure like the Golden Fleece or the Garden of the Hesperides. Above all, it's a force for life, a spiritual fervor and a creative force. It was also the symbol of the Emperor of China.

You will need…
- 1 pretty notebook
- 1 roll of transparent plastic for covering books
- 1 sewing machine and 1 bobbin of turquoise thread
- 1 box of pins
- 1 pair of dressmaking scissors and 1 pair of pinking shears
- 1 yd. double-sided satin ribbon in turquoise 1 in. wide
- 19$\frac{1}{2}$ in. double-sided satin ribbon in apple green $\frac{3}{4}$ in. wide
- 2 yd. suedette ribbon in fuchsia $\frac{1}{4}$ in. wide
- luminous embroidery thread
- a fabric Japanese cherry blossom
- some beads in rose quartz for their calming properties
- 1 little bell
- 1 mirrored ball-point pen
- 1 sheet of metallic paper for embossing

3. Cut a rectangle from the transparent plastic twice the size of your book. Slip in the dragon and, on the front, the two ribbons (the turquoise on top and the green below) leaving 2 in. of ribbon longer on the left side and the remainder on the right side (this will enable you to fix the bookmark into the book).

4. Attach them using pins (taking care to ensure that the dragon's ears are on top of the ribbons) so that they don't slip when you sew the plastic using the machine. Sew the bookmark with the machine using the turquoise thread. Part of the ribbons, as well as the dragon, are then encased in the plastic. Cut the edges of the plastic using pinking shears.

The notebook

1. Slip the turquoise ribbon over the front cover of your book in a lengthways direction. Sew to secure, sufficiently tight so that it doesn't slip off the cover.

2. Prepare several strands of luminous cotton thread around 12 in. long. Thread on your rose quartz beads and tie a knot. I always keep some rose quartz stones in my bedroom, as they symbolize inner peace and protect me while I am sleeping.

3. Sew the strands of cotton thread on to a piece of suedette ribbon, at the top and at the bottom. Sew the Japanese flower petals on to the turquoise ribbon, by sliding the ends of the threads and the ribbons into the holes in the petals. Attach everything on to the turquoise ribbon and do the same thing at the other end to attach the stones. Make some strands of luminous thread come out of the heart of the petal like a pistil.

4. To secure the book, tie your ball-point pen and your little bell on to the two ends of your suedette ribbon using a simple knot. Tie the ribbon around your book.

The simple tinkling of the bell and the action of the mirrors will quickly chase away even the smallest of your unpleasant dreams…

a window decoration

Attach these fabric "friezes" above a door or window to defend the openings to the house against spirits that could intrude.

They also evoke the latticework of the Moroccan mashrabiyas and provide protection against people looking in.

You will need...
- **fairly wide green ribbon and some finer ribbons in different colors**
- **Liberty fabric in blues and greens and in different prints**
- **coated canvas in fuchsia and turquoise blue**
- **an X-ACTO (type of mini-cutter)**
- **drawing pins**
- **a wooden drawing board**
- **pins with heads**
- **a sewing machine**
- **thread in turquoise blue**

Adjust your measurements according to the size of your window and the desired length of your garland.

1. On the reverse of the coated canvas trace some circles, rectangles and triangles around 4³/4 in. in width or diameter; then draw some motifs to be cut out.

2. Cut out each shape leaving a margin of approx. ³/4 in. for attaching it to the ribbon. Pin the shape to the wooden drawing board and cut out the motifs using the X-ACTO.

3. Cut out rectangles and strips in different widths and lengths from the Liberty fabrics. Pin them on to the ribbon alternating the different shapes. Add a fine ribbon now and again.

4. Top-stitch by machine, making sure not to sew too quickly to avoid gathering the coated canvas.

a totem bird

A totem is a plant or an animal chosen as a protective spirit and as a guide by Native American children during an initiation ritual. The totem comes to him in a vision. From then on, this animal becomes his personal guardian. It is often represented on his clothes by a portrait or a symbol, as well as on his "medicine" or "fetish" bag.

Choose your child's totem and design it in wire as a symbolic emblem to be hung above the door to their room.

How to paint the portrait of a bird
(*Paroles*, Jacques Prévert)

FIRST PAINT A CAGE
WITH AN OPEN DOOR
THEN PAINT
SOMETHING PRETTY
SOMETHING SIMPLE
SOMETHING BEAUTIFUL
SOMETHING USEFUL
FOR THE BIRD
THEN PLACE THE CANVAS AGAINST A TREE
IN A GARDEN
IN A WOOD
OR IN A FOREST
HIDE BEHIND THE TREE
WITHOUT SPEAKING
WITHOUT MOVING...
SOMETIMES THE BIRD COMES QUICKLY
BUT IT CAN ALSO
TAKE YEARS

BEFORE DECIDING
DON'T BE DISCOURAGED [...]

LES MYSTÈRES DE LA DESTINÉE
DÉVOILÉS PAR LES OISEAUX

L'ALOUETTE

Ce gentil messager du Ciel revient d'une mission de confiance de la Vierge qui est le signe du Zodiaque qui correspond au mois d'août. Et dans le grand livre du Ciel, il a pu lire votre destin. Écoutez-le vous dire à l'oreille ce qu'il a pu traduire à votre intention. Vous aimez l'argent, non pour le dépenser stupidement, mais pour les plaisirs qu'il peut vous procurer. D'ailleurs, vous pensez à vos vieux jours et songez déjà à vous constituer une réserve. Ce n'est pas un défaut. Vous ne songez pas encore à aimer. Les questions financières vous intéressent davantage. Mais rappelez-vous que l'amour est nécessaire, agréable et utile. Par lui, on connaît le bonheur.

LIBRAIRIE HAYARD, 8, rue du Croissant, PARIS

IN CHINA, THE PHOENIX IS A CHARM AGAINST ILLNESS AND EVIL.
THE SONG OF A MAGPIE IS A SIGN OF GOOD NEWS!

ALL AROUND THE WORLD, THE DOVE SYMBOLIZES PEACE.
THE ROOSTER IS A SUN SYMBOL:
ITS SONG CHASES EVIL SPIRITS OF THE NIGHT AND ANNOUNCES THE RISING OF THE SUN.

THE EAGLE
IS WITHOUT DOUBT THE KING OF BIRDS.
IT SYMBOLIZES VICTORY AND POWER FOR NATIVE NORTH AMERICANS.
WARRIORS WEAR ITS FEATHERS AS A SIGN OF BRAVERY.

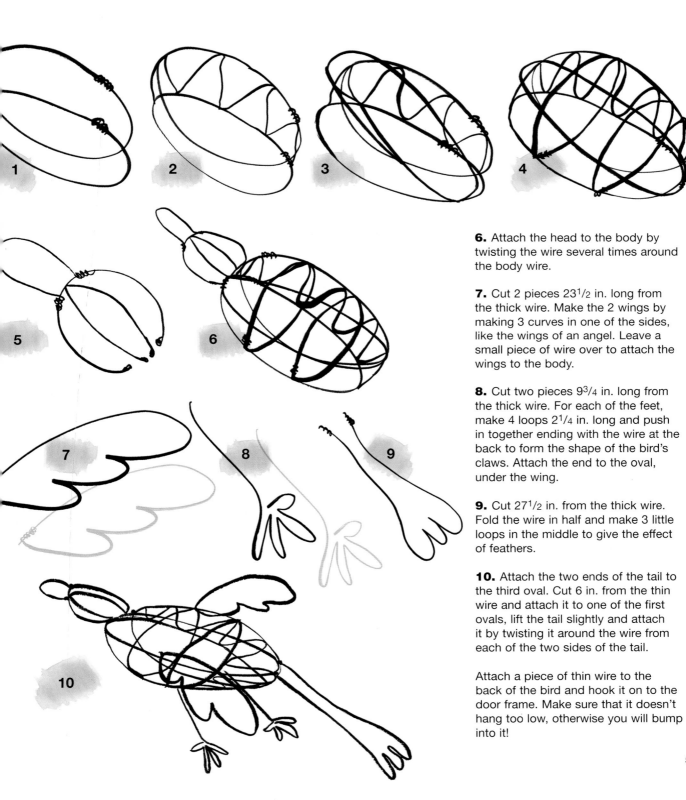

6. Attach the head to the body by twisting the wire several times around the body wire.

7. Cut 2 pieces 23$\frac{1}{2}$ in. long from the thick wire. Make the 2 wings by making 3 curves in one of the sides, like the wings of an angel. Leave a small piece of wire over to attach the wings to the body.

8. Cut two pieces 9$\frac{3}{4}$ in. long from the thick wire. For each of the feet, make 4 loops 2$\frac{1}{4}$ in. long and push in together ending with the wire at the back to form the shape of the bird's claws. Attach the end to the oval, under the wing.

9. Cut 27$\frac{1}{2}$ in. from the thick wire. Fold the wire in half and make 3 little loops in the middle to give the effect of feathers.

10. Attach the two ends of the tail to the third oval. Cut 6 in. from the thin wire and attach it to one of the first ovals, lift the tail slightly and attach it by twisting it around the wire from each of the two sides of the tail.

Attach a piece of thin wire to the back of the bird and hook it on to the door frame. Make sure that it doesn't hang too low, otherwise you will bump into it!

This lovely kit is suitable for almost any age. But if you are thinking of giving it to a child, it shouldn't be given to one under the age of 3.

an anti-nightmare and anti-worry kit

Amulets to protect babies and children, who are particularly vulnerable, have always existed throughout the world. Whether headdresses, jewelry or objects sewn on to clothes, the aim is to ward off the evil eye and to avoid illness.

But what can you do about the monsters, witches and ghosts who live in their imagination and appear whenever they go to sleep?

This playful and clever kit will prove effective against demons in any shape or form!

HOW DO YOU GET RID OF A SPRITE?
WICKED SPRITES APPEAR MAINLY AT NIGHT...
BOM-NOZ IS A NIGHTMARE SPRITE FROM FINISTÈRE IN FRANCE, WHO FALLS ON TO THE STOMACHS OF THOSE WHO SLEEP,
WILD FOULOU ATTACKS SLEEPERS BY MAKING THEM THINK THAT THEY ARE SUFFOCATING.
TO NEUTRALIZE THEM, SIMPLY TURN SOME OF YOUR CLOTHING INSIDE OUT!
THE POCKET IN YOUR PAJAMAS FOR EXAMPLE!
IF YOU CAN'T DO THAT, THEN SAY OUT LOUD!
"ILOJ ILOJ SE UT ERODA NITUL NITUL".
AND, HEY PRESTO!

A PRETTY AND EFFECTIVE KIT
A BEAR CUB AND HIS LION, ALWAYS USEFUL AGAINST BAD DREAMS
TWO LITTLE ANTI-WORRY DOLLS TO SLIP UNDER THE PILLOW BEFORE GOING TO BED
TWO SPRAYS: ONE AGAINST GHOSTS AND THE OTHER AGAINST ALL THE WICKED SPRITES
A LUMINOUS HEART, AS SMOOTH AS A PEBBLE
A LITTLE, SOFT CUSHION SPRAYED WITH PERFUME AND SOME SWEETS, TO WARD OFF ANY PANGS OF HUNGER,
ESSENTIAL TO BE ABLE TO SEE AT NIGHT, AN INDISPENSABLE TORCH...

The heart cushion

You will need…
- a 4 in. square of felt in aniseed
- an 4$^{1}/_{2}$ in. square of Liberty fabric
- embroidery thread in violet and turquoise
- a needle
- pins
- cotton wool

1. Fold over the edges of the Liberty fabric to make a 4 in. square. Place the felt square on top. Fix using pins.

2. Sew the two pieces of fabric together with the violet thread, leaving $^{1}/_{2}$ in. open. Fill with cotton wool and sew up the gap.

3. Embroider a pretty heart freehand using the turquoise thread.

4. Spray on some of your favorite perfume… Mmmm…

Anti-worry dolls

You will need…

- **scraps of colored fabric**
- **a scrap of pink felt**
- **embroidery thread in turquoise, mauve, orange and aniseed**
- **a flower bead, a fabric flower petal**
- **a needle**
- **a pair of scissors**
- **cotton wool**

The turquoise doll

1. Cut out a piece of turquoise fabric approx. $2^3/4$ x 3 in. Fold in half to make a rectangle, and stitch top/side.

2. Sew at the bottom of the rectangle using orange thread to make two little feet. Fill the rectangle using cotton wool. Edge the top of the rectangle with the aniseed thread.

3. Cut a piece of patterned fabric $1^1/4$ x $2^1/2$ in. Edge the top in mauve thread. Attach this apron to the doll $1/4$ in. from the edge, gathering it to

make the neck. Sew a flower bead to the bottom of the apron.

4. For the head, cut a 2 in. square from the pink felt and place a large cotton wool ball in the center. Sew around the square to form a ball. Push the fabric into the body and attach the head using turquoise thread.

5. With the orange thread, sew on the nose, mouth and eyes and leave some threads coming out of the head for the hair.

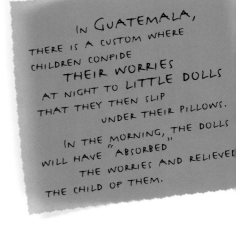

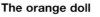

The orange doll

1. Cut a rectangle of fabric $2^1/4$ x $3^1/2$ in. Fold in half lengthways to make a rectangle 1 x $1^1/2$ in. Sew the fabric inside out, turn back the right way and fill with cotton wool, and sew the top edge with the turquoise thread.

2. As for the turquoise doll, make the head using a $1^1/2$ in. square of pink felt and attach it into the rectangle of fabric.

3. Sew the eyes, nose and mouth, attach a fabric flower petal to the top of the head, and allow several blue threads to protrude for the hair.

4. Make the waist with a small piece of suedette ribbon.

The sprays

You will need…

- **1 large and 1 small spray**
- **mint cordial**
- **orange flower water**

1. Fill the large spray with water colored with some drops of fruit cordial: so that the ghosts fly away… by spraying a few squirts into the air.

2. Fill the small spray with orange flower water: put some drops on the pillow before going to bed and say good-bye to bad dreams!

The bear cub

You will need…

- **Two 6 in. squares of orange felt**
- **a scrap of pink felt**
- **cotton wool**
- **embroidery thread in orange and turquoise**
- **1 lead pencil**
- **1 needle**
- **1 orange stick**
- **8³/₄ in. of suedette ribbon**
- **1 small bell**
- **1 little plastic lion**

1. Pin the two squares of felt together. Draw a nice bear cub on the top square. Cut out two identical bear cubs. Sew the two bear cubs edge to edge as far as the stomach using the orange thread.

2. Fill the bear cub with small pieces of cotton wool using the orange stick. Then sew the left leg and fill with cotton wool. Do the same for the right leg and finish by closing up the bear cub.

3. Cut out a little heart from pink felt. Sew it on to the bear cub.

4. Using the turquoise thread, sew the eyes, nose and mouth of the bear cub.

Arranging the case

You will need…

- **a small card hinged box (6 x 9 x 3 in.)**
- **two rectangles of fine card 2 mm thick (approx. 5 x 9 in. each)**
- **1 yd. of elastic cord**
- **adhesive ribbon, fluorescent pink, it's more fun**
- **1 wool needle**
- **1 lead pencil and a cutter**
- **a wooden drawing board**
- **some sweets (bonbons and chocolate bars)**

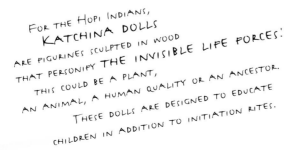

FOR THE HOPI INDIANS, KATCHINA DOLLS ARE FIGURINES SCULPTED IN WOOD THAT PERSONIFY THE INVISIBLE LIFE FORCES: THIS COULD BE A PLANT, AN ANIMAL, A HUMAN QUALITY OR AN ANCESTOR. THESE DOLLS ARE DESIGNED TO EDUCATE CHILDREN IN ADDITION TO INITIATION RITES.

1. Place your box on the card and draw around the base of the case. Turn the case over and do the same for the lid.
Retrace the outlines approx. $1/8$ in. smaller. Cut out the two pieces of card. Check that your two rectangles of card sit well in place. Re-cut them slightly if you need to.

2. Lay out the box placing the different items (dolls, sprays, etc.) in the lid and in the base. Mark the various spots for the elastic thread using a lead pencil. Make the holes using a large needle. Attach the pieces of elastic using knots on the reverse of the card.

3. Fix the two rectangles of card into the case using the adhesive ribbon. Put in the various items. And the box is ready!

thought

memoRY

trip

subliminal

mESSage

BonD

MY NOMADIC LUCKY CHARMS

INSPIRATIONS...

Leaving your home and traveling means that you are exposing yourself to all sorts of potential danger: supernatural beings, evil spirits, witches or vampires, all seeking to lead the traveler astray or to cause him harm.

This is why you need powerful talismans that you can carry while you travel.

YOU WOULD HAVE TO BE MAD TO BORROW A VEHICLE THAT WAS NOT PROTECTED BY A CHARM. WHETHER IT'S A COW, A HARNESSED HORSE, MOTORBIKE, RICKSHAW, CANOE OR TAXI, THEY ALL NEED PROTECTION: BELLS, RED POMPOMS, FABRICS, GARLANDS OF FLOWERS OR A SPARKLING CD...

The fashion of wearing lucky charms is not something new. The ethnologist and collector Lionel Bonnemère noted in his diary back in 1888 that there was a craze amongst Parisian women for among bracelets. And lucky pigs hung on rings were all the rage in 1887!

Hats and belts are clothing amulets. They protect the most sensitive parts of the body. Extra protection comes from the sewn-on triangle, which is reinforced by plaited threads. This little Turkmen boy has no chance of falling prey to an evil spirit!

A traditional ceremony in Ladakh: the men, in ceremonial dress, wear their amulets from their belt, and tied around their necks are silver cases that may contain sacred words.

63

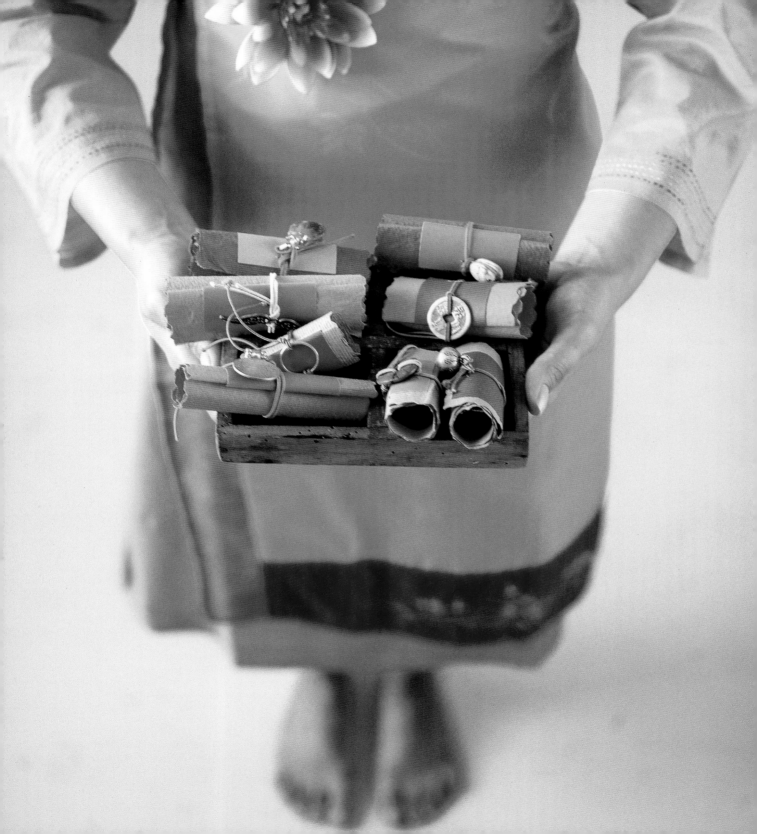

messages of good fortune

A creation in the spirit of fortune cookies…

These little cakes contain a strip of paper bearing a lucky message and were invented in the 1920s by Chinese workers in a factory in San Francisco. Nowadays, they are handed out at the end of a meal in restaurants in America.

Do the same thing by offering these little rolled-up messages to your guests!

You will need…

- **pretty sheets of paper in different colors and thicknesses**
- **some medals, lucky charms, cowry shells, stones, bells…**
- **elastic cord 3/4 in. in diameter in lots of colors**
- **a pair of pinking shears**
- **a pair of paper scissors**
- **a stapler**
- **a pen**

For each message

1. Cut a strip approx. 2³/4 in. wide from the thickest paper using the pinking shears.

2. Using the paper scissors, cut a narrower strip from the thinner paper approx. 1¹/4 in. smaller in width and length. Write your message on it (a proverb, a thought, a happy prediction, a picture, etc.).

3. Place the smaller strip on top of the larger one. Cut 13³/4 in. of elastic, fold it in half and thread your medal or bell on to it and staple the two strips and the elastic together.

4. Fold the papers, elastic and decoration in by 1¹/2 in. Roll the other end inwards with the message inside and secure the good luck message using the elastic, tying it in a simple knot. This pretty detail will delight your friends and they'll hang up this charm at home, or else they may choose to leave it rolled up and hidden under a pile of clothes so that they might stumble across it later.

"subliminal message" bookmarks

Imagine bookmarks that you can slip between the pages of a bedside book as a surprise for your friends. It's a lovely way to remind them of a memory, phrase or word that has touched them. They'll find something between the lines that will make them smile and think…

You will need…
- **transparent self-adhesive plastic**
- **colored metal wire at least 0.5 mm thick**
- **round-nosed jewelry pliers to bend the metal wire**
- **a pair of scissors**

WHAT COULD BE NICER THAN TO FIND A FORGOTTEN PHOTO, A POSTCARD OR A LITTLE MESSAGE HIDDEN BETWEEN THE PAGES OF YOUR FAVORITE BOOKS? LIKE THE WORDS OF A KINDLY FRIEND…

The heart

1. Cut 6 in. from the metal wire. Form a heart. Close the metal by twisting it. Cut.

2. Place the heart on the transparent plastic. Cut out a piece twice the size. Peel off the backing paper. Place the heart on it and fold the plastic over taking care not to wrinkle it. Smooth out well.

Love

1. Cut 6 in. from the metal wire. Fold the wire by hand to make the word "love". If necessary, use the pliers to help you shape the letters.

2. Place the word on the transparent plastic. Cut out a piece twice the size. Peel off the backing paper. Place the word on it and fold the plastic over taking care not to wrinkle it. Smooth out well.

情悄话

路边上，开了两朵小白花。
可白啦，可亮啦，
上边还有露水哩，
呵，漂亮极了的小白花！

a Korean keyring

In Korea, "Maedup" is the art of artistically tying cords of silk thread that decorate the traditional female costume; it's also a decorative element in its own right. There are 33 traditional motifs and each has its own meaning. This one is the "knot of eternity:" a powerful symbol!

A meditative and poetic piece, ideal for creating a keyring full of meaning.

IN KOREA,
THE TRADITIONAL COLORS
OF MAEDUPS ARE RED,
BLUE AND YELLOW.
NOWADAYS, OTHER COLORS CAN BE FOUND:
PINK, LIGHT GREEN, PALE AND DEEP
VIOLET AND THE COLOR JADE.

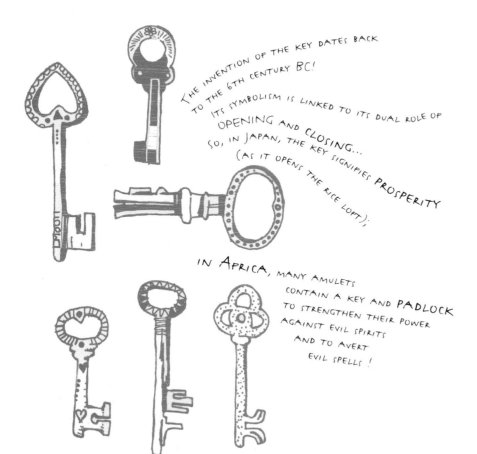

THE INVENTION OF THE KEY DATES BACK TO THE 6TH CENTURY BC!
ITS SYMBOLISM IS LINKED TO ITS DUAL ROLE OF OPENING AND CLOSING...
SO, IN JAPAN, THE KEY SIGNIFIES PROSPERITY (AS IT OPENS THE RICE LOFT);

IN AFRICA, MANY AMULETS CONTAIN A KEY AND PADLOCK TO STRENGTHEN THEIR POWER AGAINST EVIL SPIRITS AND TO AVERT EVIL SPELLS !

THE CONCEPT OF A
MAGIC KNOT IS
UNIVERSAL. WITH ITS COMPLEXITY,
THE KNOT IS MEANT TO CONFUSE
EVIL SPIRITS
AND MAKE THEM FLEE.
SIMILARLY, A PIECE OF FISHING
LINE MAY ENCOMPASS
OTHER MAGIC INGREDIENTS.

You will need…
- **32 in. of elastic cord in fluorescent pink 4mm in diameter**
- **pins with colored heads**
- **a pretty key**
- **embroidery thread in sky blue**
- **1 pin**
- **1 piece of card or a plank 9 x 12 in.**

KEEP CALM AND BREATHE DEEPLY...
AND YOU'LL SEE THAT THIS
KNOT IS NOT AS COMPLICATED
TO MAKE AS IT LOOKS!

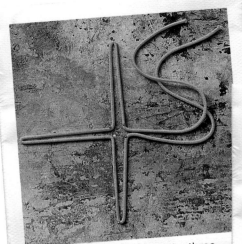

1. Fold the cord in half, make three equal loops 8 in. each. Pin the cord every 4 in. to fix it to the card.

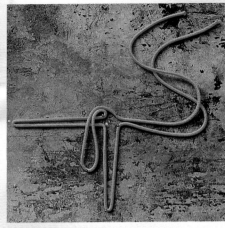

2. Remove the pin from the right loop, pass it to the left over the middle one. Fix again with the pin.

3. Remove the pin from the middle loop, pass it over the one that you have just folded over and over the one on the left. Fix again using the pin.

4. Remove the pin from the left loop.

5. Pass it over the one you have just folded over. Fix it again.

6. Take the two unfixed ends of cord and slip them into the loop of the second st by passing them over the loop that you have just fixed.

7. Pull lightly on the loops, then carefully remove all the pins and pull firmly to obtain another three loops. Fix the three loops again using the pins, as in the photo, this time with the free ends pointing upwards and bent round to make a fourth loop, and fix with pins.

8. Remove the pin from the right loop, pass it over the free ends and the lower loop towards the left and fix it with the pin.

9. Remove the pin from the lower loop, pass it over the one that you have just fixed and the left loop. Fix in place.

10. Remove the pin from the left loop. Pass it over the loop that you have just folded over and through the loop made using the free ends. Pin it.

11. Remove all the pins and pull on the loops all at the same time. Pull on the ones underneath. You will get the seven loops of the knot of eternity!

ALL YOU NEED DO NOW IS SLIP THE ENDS INTO YOUR KEY AND SECURE THEM WITH EMBROIDERY THREAD.

martisors

This piece of jewelry is a Romanian tradition.
It was given to women on March 1st and had to be worn around the wrist or hung from the lapel of a jacket until the first flowers of spring appeared. They were hung in windows in the villages of Transylvania to ward off evil spirits. Made from plaited red and white threads, they were designed to hold a coin, which, over time, has been replaced with little charms.
Create your own!

MONEY,
LIKE ANYTHING THAT SPARKLES,
ATTRACTS THE EVIL EYE
WITH ITS BRIGHTNESS AND CAN THEREFORE
DEFLECT IT MORE EASILY.
MONEY IS THE SYMBOL OF PURITY
IN THE ISLAMIC WORLD AND IN THE WEST
SMALL COINS ARE ALSO CONSIDERED
AS LUCKY CHARMS.

HOWEVER, IN
THE FAR EAST
AND IN WEST AFRICA
BRONZE AND BRASS
PERFORM THE SAME FUNCTION.

YOU CAN DESIGN SEVERAL MARTISORS AND W
THEM ALL TOGETHER.

the plaited martisor

You will need…
- **1 skein of metallic cotton embroidery thread in violet, 1 in aniseed green, 1 in turquoise blue**
- **1 "eye" pendant, 1 dove, 1 four-leafed clover**

1. Cut 3 threads 29½ in. long. Slide a pendant on to one of the threads, positioning it in the middle of the thread.

2. Measure around your wrist. Plait the two sides on either side of the pendant, taking care to stop ¼ in. from the length of half the wrist. Finish by tying a knot and cut, leaving approx. 2 in.

the crocheted martisor

You will need…

- **1 no. 4 crochet hook**
- **2 yd. of suedette ribbon 5 mm (¹/₈ in.) wide**
- **3 silver pendants**

Hold the crochet hook in the right hand, like a pencil, between your thumb and index finger, leaving the end of the hook sticking out a bit. Your left hand holds the thread and the work between the thumb and index finger and retains the thread with the little finger. (If you are left-handed, you must do the opposite and hold the work in your right hand.) This bracelet is crocheted in a small chain link.

1. To make the first link, tie a slip knot with the end of the thread. Pass the crochet hook through the loop (the knot must be very tight on the hook).

2. For the first chain link: pass the thread held in the left hand over the crochet hook catching it in the hook in the right hand (this process is called a single crochet). Carefully slip it into the first link to make a new loop and repeat the action 17 times. Thread a charm on to the ribbon, continue with 3 single crochets, slide on another charm, continue with 3 single crochets, add the last charm and continue with 17 single crochets.

3. Remove the crochet hook, slide the thread through and pull to finish the work.

a protective medallion

The medallion represents a saint or a divinity whose protection you want to invoke in certain circumstances. Sometimes it can also be replaced by a scapular, a type of pouch that was originally made from two pieces of a monk's habit and contained prayers, candle wax or leaves from consecrated branches, sewn up with red thread.

Here are some freely reinterpreted scapulars with a personal interpretation.

BUDDHIST AND SHINTOIST AMULETS FROM JAPAN RARELY SHOW THE DIVINITY THAT THEY INVOKE, EXCEPT IF IT'S DAIKOKU, WHO PROTECTS AGAINST ROAD TRAFFIC ACCIDENTS. EMBROIDERED IN GOLD THREAD, HE IS PLACED IN A TRANSPARENT POUCH AND HUNG INSIDE THE CAR.

Badges

You will need...

- **a badge-maker**
- **blank badges**
- **photos of those dearest to you**
- **sequined embroidery thread in blue, green and fuchsia**
- **1 pair of scissors**

1. Print or photocopy your photos in a format slightly larger than the size of your blank badges. Trace the outline of the image and cut out using the punch that comes with the badge-maker.

Cut out the photo. Place the badge in the receptacle of the machine. Place the photo on the badge.

2. Cut 4 in. of embroidery thread, keeping just 3 strands. Position the strands in the exact place that you would like them to be on the picture (N.B. If your montage is too thick, the machine won't work very well).

3. Place the plastic film provided in the box on to the threads and photo. Place the receptacle in the machine and then continue with the different stages as indicated in the badge-maker instructions.

Charm pouches

You will need…
- **a badge-maker**
- **fairly thick plastic freezer bags**
- **a pair of scissors**
- **safety pins**
- **pretty treasures to slip into the pouches**

1. Cut out pieces of plastic bag the size of your treasures. Slip inside pictures of those whom you want to "capture"…
Seal the 4 sides of your pouch using the machine.

2. Collect together your "charm pouches" and attach the safety pins.

3. Choose the place where you would like to hang your treasures and be reminded of them again, then close your eyes…
They will always be with you…
as soon as you pick up your bag or your jacket.

FREQUENTLY REPRESENTED ON MEDALLIONS OR STATUETTES, GANESH, THE DIVINITY WITH AN ELEPHANT'S HEAD, IS PARTICULARLY APPRECIATED BY INDIANS. HE SYMBOLIZES THE VAGARIES OF LIFE AND THE SUM OF ALL POSSIBILITIES.

a beetle amulet

An amulet is even more effective if it has been made especially for its recipient. Sometimes it contains something belonging to the person you want to protect. Native North Americans insert the umbilical cord of the newborn child into a work made from beads in the shape of a lizard that they hang on the child's cradle.

This particular amulet, inspired by this custom, may contain whatever you wish.

TURQUOISE IS A REVERED STONE FOR THE NAVAJOS, THE AMERICAN OR HIMALAYAN ZUNIS, AS ITS COLOR REFLECTS THE SKY, THE SUN AND THE POWER OF RAIN.
ITS TENDENCY TO DEVELOP A PATINA AS IT AGES MAKES IT SIMILAR TO LIFE ITSELF.
THIS STONE IS FOUND ON MANY PIECES OF AMULET JEWELRY.

You will need…

- **a pair of dressmaking scissors**
- **a 12 in. square of brown Liberty fabric**
- **cotton wool**
- **an orange stick**
- **a needle**
- **some pins**
- **embroidery cotton in chocolate brown, sky blue and gold**

- **23^1/$_2$ in. of brown suedette ribbon 2 in. wide**
- **1 glass bead ^{3}/$_4$ in. long with an African motif, 2 small turquoise glass beads, 1 small aniseed glass bead**

The body of the beetle

1. Cut a rectangle of fabric 2^3/$_4$ x 5 in. Fold in half and sew to form a rectangle 2^1/$_4$ x 1^1/$_2$ in., slightly wider at the top. Before completely closing, fill with cotton wool with the help of the orange stick.

2. Proceed in the same way with a 2 in. square of fabric. Sew it to the first part of the body.

THE BEETLE IS AN EGYPTIAN SYMBOL. IT REPRESENTS THE CYCLE OF THE SUN AND EVOKES THE STARS THAT ARE REBORN AT NIGHT. IT WAS THEREFORE CARRIED AS AN AMULET AND REPRESENTED ON THE SARCOPHAGI OF MUMMIES.

The beetle's secret pouch

Cut a ^{3}/$_4$ x 1 in. piece of fabric. Turn in the edges and sew on to the body, leaving a free edge to slip in your secret item.

The beetle's 6 legs

1. Cut 4 pieces of fabric ^{1}/$_2$ x 1 in.. Fold each one in half, turn in the edges and sew roughly. Fold in two places and top-stitch to form the joints.

2. For the front legs, proceed in the same way with 2 pieces ^{1}/$_2$ x 3 in.

3. Attach the 6 legs to the body (in the right direction) using a pin and sew on.

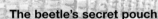

The head

Sew the large bead to the top of the body to make the head. Attach the two turquoise beads to each side at the level of the hole to make the eyes. Finish with an aniseed bead.

Decorating the body

1. Draw the motifs on the back of the beetle by embroidering the shape of the shell/wings to give an appearance of volume.

2. Make two little asymmetric circles on each of the sides and fill them in with gold thread. Also, sew the ends of the 2 front legs as if to make two gold bracelets.

To wear your amulet around your neck, attach it using some suedette ribbon, either around the neckline or letting it hang lower. And don't forget to slip your secret item into its pouch…

A LIZARD'S TAIL
WILL REGROW, EVEN IF IT IS CUT…
THIS MAKES IT
A MAGICAL ANIMAL,
OFTEN USED FOR AMULETS
AND OTHER CHARMS.

a talisman t-shirt

Some people carefully keep a photo of their loved one in their purse; others… pin them to their heart!
A nice way to carry around with you those who wish you well.

You will need…
- **a white t-shirt or nightdress**
- **black and white photocopies of photos of your loved ones in various sizes from 2– 4³/₄ in., round, square or rectangular**
- **a bottle of Transcryl (transfer product)**
- **a paintbrush**
- **a bowl**
- **a sheet of newspaper**
- **a sponge cloth and some cloths**
- **adhesive ribbon**

Preparing the transfers

1. Cut out your photocopies leaving a border around the photo of approx. ¹/₄ in.

2. Lay down the newspaper to protect your table and lay the cut-out photocopies on top.

3. Pour the transfer product into the bowl and dilute lightly with water. Paint an initial layer of the product on to the photocopy, always sweeping the paintbrush in the same direction. Leave to dry for a good 20 minutes. Paint on a second layer in the opposite direction. Repeat this process four more times crossing the layers each time.

4. Leave the last layer to dry for 48 hours.

For each photograph

1. Fill the bowl with warm water (N.B. not boiling water, otherwise you risk weakening the transfer, which could tear when you are working with it). Leave the transfer in the water for around 20 minutes so that the paper gets soaked.

2. Rub the back of the transfer with your finger to completely remove the photocopy paper. Only the transfer should remain.

3. Place the transfer flat on the sponge cloth (check the corners). Leave to dry for 24 hours.

Applying the transfers

1. Choose the places where the transfers will go and fix them using adhesive: move the pictures around until you are satisfied with the result.

2. Remove the transfers placing some sticky tape where each picture was so that you remember their places. Make sure that the garment has been well ironed.

3. For each picture, apply a layer of undiluted product to the reverse of the transfer taking care to cover the edges and corners.

Place the transfer on to the nightdress and smooth using a cloth to make sure that the product has spread evenly.

Leave to dry for a few minutes. Quickly run over with a warm iron, using a clean, thick cloth to protect the transfer.

The dragon template (p. 48)

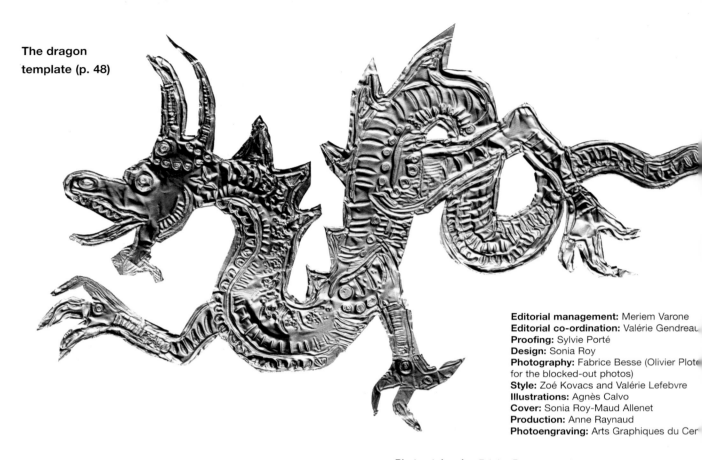

Editorial management: Meriem Varone
Editorial co-ordination: Valérie Gendreau
Proofing: Sylvie Porté
Design: Sonia Roy
Photography: Fabrice Besse (Olivier Plot
for the blocked-out photos)
Style: Zoé Kovacs and Valérie Lefebvre
Illustrations: Agnès Calvo
Cover: Sonia Roy-Maud Allenet
Production: Anne Raynaud
Photoengraving: Arts Graphiques du Cer